# Awakening
# Consciousness

by

Marc Gielissen

Available from the same author;

"Roots in the Congo"

"Why the New World Order will fail."

© 2018 by (Marc Gielissen)

ISBN-13: 978-1725570412

# Table of Contents

# **<u>Acknowledgement</u>**

I am particularly grateful for the assistance and inspiration from my spiritual guide, which considerably impacted my current life path.

I would also like to thank all those unique persons who crossed my path in this realm, people who motivated me to write about my spiritual experiences, and those who became part of my spiritual awakening.

# Introduction

Mother Earth is going through one of the most significant transformations in our known history; not only is she changing on a geophysical level, but in recent years, she is also increasing her vibrations, leading us into a higher dimension.

Humanity is on the brink of making a quantum leap into what we know as the fourth dimension, leaving our current third dimension behind. The sudden increase in consciousness, and the awakening of millions at the time, are signs that we are ready to make it happen.

Once we understand how powerful we are as light beings, a new dimension will open itself to us. There are many indications that this is happening to a considerable number of people amongst us today. Those not ready for the shift will be left behind until their vibrations are high enough to induce the transformation.

We live in times of significant change; chaos and destruction are all around us, yet, humanity is changing at an incredible speed.

Are the Schumann Resonances responsible for an increased awareness of man? What is our connection to the Universe, and how does it influence our consciousness? Are we moving into another dimension? Is our DNA changing? Do extraterrestrial beings assist us? We will address some of the burning questions in this work.

The answers you receive in this book are from another dimension; keep an open mind as the Universe is talking to you.

"A human being is a part of the whole called by us Universe, a part limited in time and space. He experiences himself, his thoughts and feeling as something separated from the rest, a kind of optical delusion of his consciousness. This delusion is a kind of prison for us, restricting us to our personal desires and affection for a few persons nearest us. Our task must be to free ourselves from this prison by widening our circle of compassion to embrace all living creatures and the whole of nature in its beauty."

**_Albert Einstein_**

# The Schumann Resonances

What are the Schumann Resonances, and why are they important to us?

Before we delve deeper into the exciting subject of our consciousness, we will examine the elements influencing or interfering with it.

In 1952, professor WO Schumann, a German physicist, hypothesised that there were measurable electromagnetic waves in the cavity between our Earth's surface and the Ionosphere.

According to Wikipedia, they are "a set of spectrum peaks in the extremely low frequency (ELF) portion of the Earth's electromagnetic field spectrum. Schumann resonances are global electromagnetic resonances, generated and excited by lightning discharges in the cavity formed by Earth's surface and the Ionosphere."

The ionosphere is our Earth's upper atmosphere, situated between 37 mi (60 km) and 620 mi (1000 km) altitude. It comprises the thermosphere and also parts of our meso — and exosphere. The whole region is ionised by solar radiation.

The inner edge of the magnetosphere, the ionosphere, is essential in the propagation of radio waves, made possible by the presence of atmospheric electricity. Besides the propagation of radio waves, scientists discovered that they also substantially impact all living organisms on Earth. The ionosphere is also where we find the fantastic auroras or northern lights. (Aurora Borealis) They are formed when charged particles from the sun penetrate the Earth's magnetic field; this occurs during solar flares. When the particles collide with atoms and molecules in our atmosphere, they create photons. (countless light bursts)

The Schumann Resonance can be considered a planetary wave generated by the upper layers of our atmosphere. Lighting feeds our planet with extremely low frequency (ELF) waves. After research, Schumann observed that the negatively charged Earth interacts with the positively charged ionosphere and concluded that Earth has a heartbeat. He was the first scientist to acknowledge that the phenomenon created a belt that controls life's pulse on this planet.

Scientists are using the Schumann Resonances to observe global lightning activity and measure global temperature and variations of water vapour in the upper troposphere. They even found a way to predict earthquakes by measuring geomagnetic and ionospheric disturbances.

In 1993 ER William suggested that, after showing a correlation between the resonance frequency and tropical air temperature, the Schumann Resonances could also be used to measure global warming.

Dr Luc Montagnier, a French virologist, involved in discovering the human immunodeficiency virus, used a homoeopathic routine to dissolve bacterial DNA into the water with dilutions high enough to eliminate every single DNA molecule from the sample. He exposed a separate clean water sample and the diluted sample to the Schumann Resonance. (ultra low-frequency belt) His experiment showed that water is not only able to retain but also transmit DNA information when subjected to a specific frequency, a fantastic discovery. It shows how it can influence our whole being and, even more — everything around us.

The more scientists explore the world of frequencies, the more they discover how important they are to all organisms in the universe.

Further scientific literature suggests that ambient electromagnetic fluctuations, such as the ones we find in geomagnetic activity, may affect our physiology and psychology and result in a positive association between geomagnetic activity and systolic (S) and diastolic (D) blood pressure (BP). Cherry R. suspects in a study from the Hokkaido Institute of Public Health that the Schumann resonance propagated by ELF waves is the possible biological mechanism that explains the natural and human health effects of geomagnetic activity.

The findings of Cherry R. (Schumann Resonance, a plausible biophysical mechanism for the human health effects of solar — geomagnetic activity.), in her study on the subject, were remarkable, as she showed that there is a direct association between disease-related illness and health-related issues, body mass index, quality of life, and even depression. In any case, it is clear to the international scientific community that exposure to low-frequency, low-intensity electromagnetic fields can produce biological effects.

The existence and effects of the Schumann Resonances are not limited to planet earth but, according to various scientists, influence other celestial objects. Energy and vibrations are all around us and are the building blocks for what we perceive as reality.

It's interesting to know that two critical factors influence the Schumann Resonances on other planets and moons:

1.  A closed, planetary-sized, and approximately spherical cavity consisting of conducting lower and upper boundaries separated by an insulating medium.

2.  A source of electrical excitation of electromagnetic waves in the ELF range.

More recently, Fernando Simoes, a scientist at NASA's Goddard Space Flight Center in Greenbelt, Md, made a remarkable observation. He discovered that the Schumann Resonance could also be observed in space. According to Simoes, *"researchers didn't expect to observe these resonances in space, but it turns out that energy is leaking out, and this opens up many possibilities to study our planet from above."*

Scientists are only scratching the surface when it comes to an understanding the influence of the Schumann Resonances on our earth's environment, all the celestial objects surrounding it, and last but not most diminutive, all living beings.

Our knowledge is limited by the dimension we live; the higher our consciousness, the more we will understand.

As humans, we are pure energy forms, each generating its magnetic field. Therefore, it is no surprise that frequency variations heavily influence us.

We will further discover why the resonances significantly impact our central nervous system and are essential to developing our consciousness. They are probably the main reason we feel better when we are away from cities and the mad rat race, something most of us experience. The city negatively influences our brain due to constant exposure to traffic, crowds, and a stressed environment. All those elements are interfering with the treatment and healing abilities of nature. Many of us have lost contact with Mother Earth for a long time.

In quantum physics, we know that every substance, including human cells, emits a unique electromagnetic "fingerprint." Dr Fritz Popp, a German biophysics researcher, scanned photons in living examples when he was trying to understand the nature of the energy field that surrounds all living matter.

During his research, Dr Popp discovered that animals and plants emit light as bio-photons from the cellular nuclei. He found that the cells work like rain transmitters and receivers; they exchange information. Popp also measured coherence, which is the level of correlation between distinct frequencies of the cells. He concluded that high coherence indicated healthy cells and low coherence signs of disease. In the following chapters, we will discover why they are so crucial to our wellness and, most of all, our spiritual growth.

# Mother Earth's heartbeat is changing.

For a very long time, Mother Earth's natural heartbeat was measured at 7.83 Hz, a frequency that was called OM by the ancient Indian Rishis. They were known as "seers," "great sadhus", or "sages," who, after intense meditation (tapas), realised the supreme truth and eternal knowledge. Their findings were later expressed in hymns and used in different cultures and religions.

For many years the resonance frequency has been steady at 7.83 Hz, with only tiny registered variations. This relative status quo would suddenly change when the Russian Space Observing System registered an essential change in the frequency, starting from June 2014, when something remarkable happened. The monitors of the observing system showed a sudden spike in activity, measuring frequencies up to 8.5 Hz. The same Russian Space Observatory even recorded days when the Schumann Resonances accelerated to 16.5 Hz. It would become the start of significant changes to the Schumann Resonance.

Scientists were baffled by their findings as this had never happened before since they started measuring the resonances. They first suspected an equipment failure, but later tests confirmed nothing was wrong with it.

The Schumann Resonances interact or influence humans because they connect our hearts and the earth's electromagnetic field. As mentioned before, we have our magnetic field and are connected to everything surrounding us.

According to Dr Kathy Forti, a clinical psychologist and author of several scientific papers and books, the Schumann Frequency is said to be "in tune" with the human brain's alpha and theta states. She further explains that a 7.83 Hz frequency is an alpha/theta state, a relaxed yet dreamy state of neutral idling. It can be defined as a state in which we are just waiting for something to happen. In other words, humanity was kept in a dream state for a very long time, but this is changing now.

The frequencies from 8.5 to 16.5 Hz are moving us out of the above-mentioned theta range into a calmer alpha state with faster, more alert beta frequencies starting to appear. The increase would correlate with slowly waking up cognitively.

Dr Forty said that 12 - 15 Hz in neurofeedback is called Sensory-Motor Rhythm frequency (SMR). It's an ideal state of "awakened calm." Our thought processes are more transparent and focused, yet we are still "in the flow" or "in the now." In other words, Mother Earth is shifting her vibrational frequency, and so are we. This is one of the many signs that we are AWAKENING.

Nikola Tesla revealed that; *"Alpha waves in the human brain are between 6 and 8 hertz. The frequency of the human activity resonates between 6 and 8 hertz. All biological systems operate in the same frequency range. The human brain's alpha function is in this range, and the electrical resonance of the earth is between 6 and 8 hertz. Thus, our entire biological system — the brain and the earth—works on the same frequencies. If we can control that resonate system electronically, we can control the entire mental system of humanity."*

Tesla was one of the first persons to point out that changing the frequencies could change the behaviour of humans. This is happening to us today; we are all enslaved in a system that uses us rather than allowing us to grow our full potential as light beings. The awakening is a significant event in our spiritual evolvement and part of our potential to ascend into higher dimensions. It is clear that Tesla was well aware of what was happening but was silenced.

Scientists report that the Earth's magnetic field, which directly impacts the Schumann Resonance, has been slowly weakening for the past 2,000 years, with a significant decline in the last few years.

Lewis B. Hainsworth, an Australian electrical engineer, was among the first to suggest that human health is linked to a geophysical framework through the naturally occurring Schumann ELF (extremely low frequencies). According to his theory, naturally occurring features determine the frequency spectrum of human brain-wave rhythms. His findings were that frequencies of human brain waves evolved in response to these signals.

Hainsworth has said, *"As human beings, we have extraordinary potentials we have hardly begun to study, much less understand. Creative gifts, intuitions and talents that are unpredictable or emergent may stabilise in generations to come. Hopefully, we can learn to understand our emergence from an essentially electromagnetic environment and facilitate our potential for healing, growth and non-local communication."*

Research shows that everything is connected by magnetic and electromagnetic fields, giving sufficient evidence that all changes will immediately influence every single element of our perceived reality, including our body.

Different cultures are revealing the reason behind the existence of our magnetic field. One of the most exciting theories is an old sage from India who claimed that the earth's magnetic field was put in place by the "Ancient Ones" to block our primordial memories of our true heritage. It was considered a way to give us free will, unhampered by memories.

Due to the changes we experience in our magnetic field today, those memory blocks are slowly loosening. It's one of the elements responsible for helping us raise our consciousness, enabling us to see the truth about our purpose and objectives here on earth. We will finally understand who we are. The veil is lifting; the blinders are coming off, and we are collectively awakening. The distorted energy field in which we lived for a very long time will be restored, and we will once again be aligned with the higher energy sources that will allow us to grow spiritually.

To better understand what is causing this sudden global rise in consciousness, we need to dig deeper into some aspects not covered by the mainstream media and even hidden by most scientists. Despite clear signs around us, people still keep their heads in the sand and ignore all warnings under the pretext that what we will discover next is just a "conspiracy theory."

The sudden increase in the Schumann Resonances is directly related to the approach of our binary twin star "Nemesis," accompanied by its system of moons and planets. It's a natural event which occurs approximately every 3,600 years, an appearance documented by several ancient civilisations, the most important being the Sumerians. They were the first Mesopotamian civilisation that lived from about 3000BC to 1200BC in a region known as Iraq today. It's not a coincidence that they invented written language, the wheel, irrigation, and the first justice system.

The Epic of Gilgamesh, written by the Sumerians, is considered the world's oldest book. They were also the first civilisation to build cities and establish monarchies and bureaucracies, almost as we know them today — just to mention a few of their accomplishments. They were a very advanced civilisation with extended mathematics, science and astronomy knowledge.

Interestingly, gods ruled those cities through a priest-king who exercised divine authority. The Sumerian civilisation was ruled by beings not from this earth, much more advanced than we can imagine, even by our current standards. We briefly mention them because they are essential in leaving us a message of what to expect in our immediate future.

It was the author Zecharia Sitchin, who spent a significant amount of time translating the Sumerian tablets, who suggested that he found clear evidence of the existence of the 12th planet in our solar system.

The Sumerians wrote about a planet or sun with an elongated, 3,600-year-long elliptical orbit around our sun. It's a brown dwarf star known as "Nemesis." The event is covered or followed by many people on social media because, as mentioned before, mainstream media and most scientists just keep silent.

We will not dig deeper into the subject in this book. Still, it's an integral part of the elements responsible for our increased consciousness, experienced by millions today.

# Our connection with the universe

There is an essential interaction between our body, which also emits an electromagnetic field on its own, and all other heavenly bodies in the universe. Our heart emits the most extensive electromagnetic field of all the organs in our body. Scientific research confirms that as we practice coherence while radiating love and compassion, the heart generates a coherent electromagnetic wave which enhances social coherence.

The more individuals radiating heart coherence, the stronger the energy field becomes. This energetic field will allow us to alter our environment by generating positive thoughts and feelings. Research results also confirm that our electromagnetic field is directly connected to Mother Earth and the rest of the universe. It means that in the core of our being, we are ONE with the Earth on which we live, the universe, or rather multiverse, and God, or whatever name different cultures give to the omnipresence of the light and love being of pure energy.

The true meaning of ONENESS is that we can influence the universe, and the universe can affect us. According to Dr Rozman, heart coherence is *"an alignment within and amongst systems — whether quantum particle, organisms, human beings, social groups, planets or galaxies. This harmonious order signifies a coherent system whose optimal functioning is directly related to the ease and flow in its processes."*

In other words, generating "positive emotions," such as love, appreciation, and gratitude, will directly affect our nervous system and influence the people, fauna, and flora around us. The impact is much more significant than we can imagine, as the moment we spread love through the universe, instantly, we are altering our direct and even indirect environment positively. What we think and feel will create the reality in which we live.

Albert Einstein once said in 1920 that; *"there is no atom, there is only field."* It means that nothing exists outside of the field; there is only the field. Our sun, the stars, and the planets are all part of our body, which cannot exist without them. The veil of sensory illusion conceals what we call consciousness, giving us the impression of being separated from our environment. In reality, we are an integral and inseparable part of it. Our connection to the universe is difficult to understand from the third dimension.

We have the illusion of being close to our body and at a considerable distance from the universe around us; only when we become awake do we realise that this perceived distance is non-existing. When we start thinking in spiritual terms, there is no time or space; we are the universe itself.

The Native Americans, African tribes, and the Aboriginals understood the importance of our connection to the moon, sun, stars and Mother Earth. As spirit beings, they identified that the relation was non-physical and that material belonging was only a temporary creation in this plane. In contrast, our spiritual being has no limitations in what it can achieve.

Mudrooroo, a nal writer, once mentioned, *"Our spirituality is a oneness and an interconnectedness with all that lives and breathes, even with all that does not live or breathe."* It resumes it all.

What is happening to our society today?

The greedy world we live in today revolves around material possessions and power over others. It became an egocentric consumerist world, which lost all connection with nature. Humanity is at a crossroads, as it received a precious gift from the universe where it is offered the opportunity to make drastic changes to the way of life, how we treat Mother Earth, and all that makes part of it.

We are allowed to return to a state of a light being, which is what we initially were. A being that is not controlled and enslaved by dark forces. In the book *"Why the New World Order will fail"*, the reader will find out how and why we came to this point in our existence. Exposing what is happening in the world and understanding why it is happening is an integral part of the awakening process, leading humanity into an era and dimension of increased consciousness.

Negativity around us is hampering our spiritual growth, but once again, the universe is giving us a chance to wake up from a long and deep sleep. It is up to each individual to take the opportunity to raise their consciousness or continue learning in the three-dimensional environment we live in today. Humanity has been gifted with free will to evolve or not.

# What is consciousness?

Before we go into the spiritual side of consciousness, we will look more closely at what scientists have to say about the subject.   As we know, they are always driven by objective, measurable data to conclude their findings.

According to Christof Koch, the chief scientist and president of the Allen Institute for Brain Science in Seattle, consciousness is everything you experience.  He states, "*it is the tune stuck in your head, the sweetness of chocolate mousse, the throbbing pain of a toothache, the fierce love for your child and the bitter knowledge that eventually all feelings will end.*"

He refers to the experiences mentioned above as "qualia." Although many scientists deny that qualia exist or that it can ever be meaningfully studied by science, most scholars accept consciousness as a given. However, they are still trying to understand its relationship to the objective world in which scientists need to describe it.  They want to avoid the philosophical discussions and instead connect them to a highly excitable part of brain matter, which is giving rise to consciousness, according to their observations.

The author would like to clarify that when we talk about consciousness in this work, we don't allude to the medical state of a person or patient but the more complex spiritual state of awareness.

It's clear that, regardless of what scientists try to observe and explain, consciousness is a state of awareness in which we experience wakefulness and connect with our soul. It cannot be explained mechanistically, as it is beyond the physical form. It's the main reason why machines and robots will never be able to possess consciousness, regardless of how intelligent and sophisticated they might be.

In our three-dimensional world, we have a false impression that matter creates our environment, but in reality, this perception is distorted by our belief system. In contrast to what we perceive, our ability to use mental power enables us to create our existence and the matter generated by thoughts. This concept is difficult to grasp from our limited viewpoint. Scientists are struggling with it, but some philosophers have a better explanation. Consciousness is how we view ourselves as an observer, an entity disconnected from the body and mind and fully aware of the essence of "being." We can be our judge and look at our actions or even thoughts from a distance. The Latin word "*Conscientia*" comes close to a good description, as it means moral conscience. It was first used by *Marcus Tullius Cicero, who was a Roman statesman, orator, lawyer and philosopher,* in Latin juridical texts, and later by *Renè Descartes,* a French philosopher, mathematician, and scientist, who used the word "conscience" as the "search after truth."

We have two forms of consciousness; self-consciousness, a state in which we are aware of what is happening to us as a person, and global consciousness, created by the interaction and thoughts of all living beings in the universe.

The scientific world is eager to investigate what consciousness is and how it not only influences people but the entire environment surrounding them.

The recently developed quantum theory confirms that nothing is natural for us until perceived by the observer. Max Plank said, "*science cannot solve the ultimate mystery of nature. And that is because, in the last analysis, we are part of the mystery we are trying to solve.*"

Some scientists would explain that consciousness is to humans as the "cloud" is to computers, an external database containing all information. According to Penrose Hameroff's Orchestrated Objective Reduction Model, "*Consciousness is a process in the structure of the universe, connected to the brain via quantum computations in microtubules.*"

The author is convinced that we are all connected to the "one source" of global consciousness, a source we can tap into when our vibrational level is high enough. Consciousness is the energy that connects "all there was, is, and ever will be."

We can conclude that global consciousness is the intuitively perceived knowledge and energy sourced from a web throughout the universe, connecting us all as ONE. It is precisely that state of global consciousness which will be further discussed in this work. Before we dig deeper into the matter, the writer would like to show you some interesting scientific data.

The information collected from different reliable scientific sources indicates a clear correlation between consciousness and our connection to the universe, which comprises everyone and everything.

The Global Consciousness Project (GCP) is an example of how more than 100 scientists worldwide explore whether the construct of interconnected consciousness can be scientifically validated through objective measurement. The organisation collected data covering different experiments over 35 years, and their findings are pretty amazing.

In the Journal of Scientific Exploration, Peter Bancel and Roger Nelson from GCP explain that; *"the Global Consciousness Project measures the output deviation of a global network of physical random number generators (RNGs) at the time of major world events. The project hypothesises that the coherent attention or emotional response of large populations induced by the events will correspond to characteristic deviations of the network output."*

The findings of the Global Consciousness Project are exciting and support the thesis of oneness, which philosophers from different cultures and time frames suggested. They communicated this: *"We don't yet know how to explain the correlations between events of importance to humans and the GCP data, but they are quite clear. They suggest something akin to the image held in almost all cultures of unity or oneness, based on an interconnection that is fundamental to life.*

*Our efforts to understand these complex and interesting data may contribute insight into the role of the mind as a creative force in the physical world. We can hope they will encourage awakening to conscious evolution."*

An exciting fact observed by the same team of scientists is that they found a substantial correlation between the CGP measurements and solar cycle counts. We also know that our sun is developing more sunspots than before, significantly impacting us. The effect on earth is that more solar flares and coronal mass ejections (CMEs) influence all life on earth. These same CMEs and solar flares can send enormous amounts of charged particles and energy into our atmosphere. The same phenomenon is also responsible for a significant increase in the Schumann Resonances, which directly influence our whole being and state of consciousness.

Recent findings in quantum science confirm that we always existed and always will exist. According to Dr David Hamilton, who has a PhD in organic chemistry, consciousness has always been in the universe through quantum particles; that's why, when you are born, it's just channelled into a physical being. He concluded, *"Each of us is pure consciousness, currently focused in a physical dimension."*

Albert Einstein said: *"Energy cannot be created or destroyed; it can only be changed from one form to another."* He was not alone in his findings about consciousness; Dr Robert Lanza, an American medical doctor and scientist, also believes that our minds exist through energy in our physical body. When we die, the energy of that consciousness will continue to exist on a quantum level.

According to Professor Bernard Carr from Queen Mary University in London, *"Our consciousness interacts with another dimension. Our physical sensors only show us a three—dimensional universe...What exists in the higher dimensions are entities we cannot touch with our physical sensors."*

As we move through our different states of consciousness, we discover a variety of parallel worlds and beings. The only constant we have will be the connection with all worlds and beings in the multiverse.

# The new earth

While millions on earth are worried about the impact of a pole shift, triggering significant ecological and geographical changes, others are confident that they will move into another dimension and escape the physical turmoil we live in today. Will we experience a new mass extinction event soon, or is something else happening to us?

According to the Australian Aboriginals, we are all visitors to this time, in this place. We are just passing through; our purpose is to observe, learn, grow and love, after which we return home. Our subjective observation is that our current earth is, and has always been, our home — a place we only leave when we die. The reality might be entirely different when we look at it from a multidimensional spiritual angle. When we realise how we are connected to everything that was, is, and ever will be, our perception will change, and we will know that our current earth is only a stepping stone to another place in the space-time continuum of the multiverse. Some people have the impression that they don't belong to this earth but rather have their roots in other planets or a parallel world. The reality, however, is that we all belong to all worlds simultaneously, a difficult concept to grasp.

What to expect in our immediate future?

December 21, 2012, was the last day and year in the Mayan calendar; it wasn't the end of the world as many wrongly interpreted, but rather the end of a consciousness era in our space-time continuum. A fact which was well known by the ancient Mayan civilisation but misunderstood by many. It would be the start of our ascension into a higher vibrational dimension. Many end-of-time scenarios are only based on fear-mongering manipulation in an attempt to block the ascension and keep us in a lower third-dimensional realm. Still, we know with certitude today that this universal ascension cannot be stopped.

Not all of us will make a move from the "Third dimension" (our current physical earth) to the "Fourth or fifth Dimension" (the more spiritual world). Only those who found the light within themselves, people who are spiritually awake and fully aware of the fact that they are light beings connected to the universe, will participate in the shift.

Those not open to spiritual growth will be an opportunity to learn further and experience the third dimension until their souls are ready to ascent.

The transformation humanity is undergoing now is not of a physical but of pure spiritual nature. It's not coming from the outside; it can only be found within our core. We are all experiencing an extraordinary time in space, a time in which the current third dimension will take place for an entirely new world.

Most souls on earth will make the voyage into a higher level of consciousness, a state of awareness that will even change our DNA's structure. For many of us, the third dimension, with all the karma comprising it, will be dissolved soon. We will be living in a physically less-dense environment, which will give us opportunities to grow further to a state of enlightenment. (the reunification with the one Devine source)

Not only are we humans changing, but Mother Earth is also changing; the recent significant increase in the Schumann Resonances is a sign that we are receiving considerable vibrational upgrades; it's all happening right now. It also means that we humans are changing and our earth with everything connected to it. We can expect very soon to live in a new peaceful, and aligned world.

Remember that there is no separation in the universe; all changes will impact each part of the whole. All beings, dimensions and time periods are interconnected.

If we look into what is happening in the world today, we can recognise the signs of the consciousness shift. The fourth dimension is a dimension of reality; it's the link between our physical and spiritual reality. The change doesn't come easy; the earth experiences significant floods, earthquakes, volcano eruptions and fires, and we as a society are on the brink of complete chaos. Morals are lost, our community society is absorbed by war and greed, and fear is the ultimate tool to keep our vibrations low.

Despite all the above, millions of people are opening their eyes and seeing the large-scale corruption, control and deception around them. The evil plans of the elite are no longer hidden; secret societies are forced to disclose what they have been hiding from us for a very long time. The truth is forced on them, and there is nothing able to stop a full disclosure. The shift is a reality; we can observe all the signs around us today; it is happening now and fast.

Our reality is shifting; many things we believed to be true yesterday are no longer perceived as legitimate today. We can see and experience things we never saw before because our reality is slowly shifting into a higher dimension. To know if you are ready for the ascension of consciousness, you could answer the questions below;

Is your intuition stronger than ever before?

Why are you attracted to spirituality?

Did you notice that animals are less scared of you?

Why are you so eager to know the truth today?

Do you feel connected to nature again?

Are you walking away from the materialistic world?

Is there a shift in your thoughts, values and beliefs?

Is your ego slowly moving aside?

Are you less attached to possessions or positions?

Is religion making a place for spirituality?

If you show any of the above signs, you are on the right path to your next increased consciousness level. Our reality is changing, and you are this reality's (part) creator. The way we think and project as a group will define the environment in which we live.

Forget all about the material world — welcome into the spiritual world. We have the opportunity to leave this space-time dimension and "incarnate" in higher dimensions; however, not all of us will take this decision. Although the earth is moving into a higher dimension, some of us will not choose to participate in the "ascension," mainly because our souls are not ready for it.

Every individual has the choice to proceed to a higher frequency or remain in the current space-time dimension until their souls are ready. It's a long road through dimensional incarnations, and some souls are not prepared to incarnate into the higher vibrational dimensions; they will need more time to increase their consciousness level.

As our earth is moving into a higher frequency, the consciousness level in the current third dimension will automatically be increased, in tune with the new Schumann Resonances. It means that the third dimension we live in today will not be the same as the one we will be experiencing tomorrow. Whether souls want to stay in the third dimension or move onto the higher dimensions, humanity will experience a "Universal Ascension."

Before we elaborate on the subject, the reader should know that we live in a "multiverse," comprising many different levels or dimensions.

Our earth, as well as everything surrounding it, has different dimensions. Every single dimension of the 12 known universal dimensions has its own motion, spin, oscillation and space-time. They all have their own physical reality and exist independently from each other, although there is a connection and even an overlapping sometimes. Important to know is that, like with everything else in the universe, they are all interconnected and part of our levels of consciousness ascension.

Ascension is a universal evolutionary process applicable to every soul, solar system and galaxy; it is part of the global universal dimension. This universal dimension contains higher and lower dimensional levels, in which the frequencies gradually increase until they reach the "GOD" source.

## Our Multi-Dimensional Universe

We should ask ourselves the question if higher dimensions exist at all. Many people classify the idea of those unseen worlds as belonging to science fiction writers, mystics or even charlatans. Even though we are talking about manifestations beyond, what we consider the customary laws of physics, many serious theoretical physicists not only believe they exist but are responsible for many unknown phenomena in nature.

There are no coincidences in life; it should be understood that all events in history are linked or related. We can therefore state with confidence that time, dimensions, and beings are all interconnected. Our soul has the experience of many lifetimes and is as multidimensional as the universe itself. Hidden dimensions and unseen realms make up a much larger part of the universe than what we can physically perceive by our limited three-dimensional vision. Physicists call the unseen realms "dark energy" or "dark matter."

Dark matter is an exciting example of the mystery surrounding us; thought to account for approximately 85% of the matter in the universe, scientists are unable to say precisely what it contains or what its function is. At least they concluded that what they saw as empty space is not "empty" at all. According to Wikipedia, most dark matter is considered non-baryonic, possibly composed of some undiscovered subatomic particles.

In Albert Einstein's gravity theory, he predicted that empty space could possess its own energy. The author is convinced that Einstein was one of the few who could tap into the Akashic Records (we will discuss this subject later) and have a glimpse of the unknown elements of the universe. The most influential inventions, or discoveries, as Nikola Tesla once said, came during dreams or moments of heightened intuition.

Unfortunately, limitations in our third-dimensional realm disabled them from accessing full knowledge of the matter. This is also why Einstein often alluded to the fact that the more scientific knowledge we acquire, the more we are aware that, in reality, we know nothing. We must realise that science, at our current level, will never be able to explain the mysteries of the universe.

The famous Dr Michio Kaku, an American theoretical physicist professor, futurist, and populariser of science, who is a professor of theoretical physics at the City College of New York and CUNY Graduate Center, gave an interesting example of how limited our perception of the world can be when he explained how a carp (fish) would perceive reality.

Dr Kaku; *"I would ask myself a question only a child could ask: what would it be like to be a carp? What a strange world it would be! I imagined that the pond would be an entire universe, one that is two-dimensional in space. The carp would only be able to swim forwards and backwards, and left and right. But I imagined the "up" concept beyond the lily pads would alienate them. Any carp scientist daring to talk about "hyperspace," i.e. the third dimension "above" the pond, would immediately be labelled a crank. I wondered what would happen if I could reach down and grab a carp scientist and lift it into hyperspace. I thought what a wondrous story the scientist would tell the others! The carp would able on about unbelievable new laws of physics: Beings who could emit sounds without bubbles. I then wondered: how would a carp scientist know about our existence? One day it rained, and I swath rain drops forming gentle ripples on the surface of the pond."*

# Then I understood

*The carp could see rippling shadows on the surface of the pond. The third dimension would be invisible to them, but vibrations in the third dimension would be clearly visible. These ripples might even be felt by the carp, who would invent a silly concept to describe this, called "force." They might even give these "forces" cute names, such as light and gravity. We would laugh at them because, of course, we know there is no "force at all, just the rippling of the water."*

Unfortunately, our scientists can't give a conclusive answer to the questions raised, although theoretical physics predicts that more dimensions should exist in our invisible space. We must look into ancient knowledge and spirituality to find some explanations.

We can assume that there are an undefined number of parallel universes in which the higher dimensions increase in volume as they come closer to the source. As in Dr Kaku's story about the carp, we can only understand and explain what is visible to us. Once we learn how to use our spiritual abilities and look beyond matter, we will discover a whole new unexplored world for us, three-dimensional beings.

In an ancient Hindu text, Vishnu Purana states: *"This universe, composed of seven zones, is everywhere swarming with living creatures, large or small...so there is not the eighth part of an inch in which they do not abound."*

We will not find those planes or zones at different physical locations; they all occupy the same space, only in other dimensions.

There are differences in the number of solar planes or dimensions described in various works of literature. Still, they all share that the higher planes are much more subtle (energy) and the lower planes denser (physical). Besides the seven planes we mentioned above, there are several sub-planes. In some ancient texts, we can even find a total of 49 planes, seven planes, each comprising seven sub-planes. The reality, however, is that despite what many claims to be exact, we at our level in the consciousness evolution cannot fully understand the higher dimensions in a 3-dimensional environment. Only through spiritual guidance can we glimpse what is waiting for us after our consciousness level is at a higher frequency.

Some exceptions exist; those with unique gifts can move from one dimension to another. Most of them reached a form of enlightenment through meditation.

We should be in the 3:7 plane, moving into the 4:1 plane. It means that we are raising our consciousness level from a mental plane (3) into the unity plane (4) and evolving towards the spiritual plane (5). Beings from higher planes have access to the lower planes because they are subtle energy-matter. It's tough for lower-plane beings to access the higher dimensions without first increasing their vibrational level. Only spiritual guidance can give us information about the higher dimensions.

Our perception of reality is only what we experience and see; that's why it is so persistent. Our third dimension is only a subjective illusion and therefore distorts our understanding of who we are, what we are doing here, and last but not least, why we are in this dimension. It's tough for us to grasp what is beyond our visual and sensory perceived reality.

We could compare our reality with a radio that only gives us one channel to listen to. If we never looked for other media, it would always give us the same program and be our only available station. In contrast, once we find a way to look beyond and change channels, we see a multitude of different programs, some we never heard of before. A new world opens to us while still being in the exact physical location; isn't that amazing?

There is a fascinating experiment done by Professor Dr David Bohm, one of the most significant theoretical physicists of the 20th century, a scientist who contributed new ideas to quantum theory, neuropsychology, and philosophy of mind. In his experiments with particles, which make up matter in the form of humans, or any material objects, he discovered that they are projections of a higher-dimensional reality, which cannot be accounted for in terms of any force or interaction between them. His central theory was; *"the unbroken wholeness of the totality of existence as an undivided flowing movement without borders."*

Prominent physicists such as Max Planck and Albert Einstein forwarded the idea long ago that matter, the way we perceive it, does not exist. Albert Einstein stipulated that; *"concerning matter, we have been all wrong. What we have called matter is energy, whose vibration has been so lowered as to be perceptible to the senses. There is no matter."*

Niels Bohr, a Danish physicist and Nobel Prize winner known for his model of atomic structure (Bohr model), claimed that; *"Everything we call real is made of things that cannot be regarded as real. If quantum mechanics hasn't profoundly shocked you, you haven't understood it yet."*

Dr Robert Lanza mentioned that: *"there are an infinite number of universes, and everything that could possibly happen occurs in some universe."*

An illusory perception guides us, only shaped by fragmentary thoughts. In reality, there is only oneness in a multidimensional space-time consciousness.

Are we currently shifting into a higher frequency?

There is convincing evidence that we are shifting or at least a high number of people amongst us. Humanity is moving into the fourth dimension at an astonishing and unprecedented speed today. Old beliefs are tumbling fast; what seemed to be true yesterday is no longer true today; we live in turbulent times. There is a movement to disclose all the evil practices around us, and many political and even church leaders are questioned about their actions. In general, corruption and acts against humanity are exposed like never before.

Our reality is about to shift from a purely physical into a more spiritual dimension. Millions of people in a state of deep sleep are awakening today, realising that they need to change their old belief systems and prepare for a vital consciousness shift.

To benefit from the global spiritual growth, which is only made possible by a burst of energy coming from the universe, we need to align our vibrations with those of the new world.

Humanity is changing at an incredible speed; our consciousness is evolving into a higher vibrational state, a condition in which we can see things we never saw before and do things we never could ever have imagined.

Slowly we will find our true spiritual power again and return to a state of "light being," which is our original state of being. Humanity is slowly awakening from a very long and deep sleep, a sleep in which we were mind controlled. Most of us were, and some still are, in a state of subconscious dream, in which we look at events from the past or those still to happen in the future. Unfortunately, we rarcly find ourselves in the present moment, which is the actual state.

We are always looking behind us, complaining about what happened to us, after which we look into the future to find happiness and fulfilment to compensate for what happened in the past. Very seldom are we aware that being in the present is the only place that will give us self-awareness?

With the mass awakening happening right now, our self-awareness is increasing daily. We can see things we never saw before and become aware of our inner world of emotions, feelings and thoughts. Even science is suddenly moving forward with recent discoveries, such as the "supersymmetric string theory," which explains how all of the particles and fundamental forces in nature are based on vibrations of tiny supersymmetric strings. Although still without any conclusive scientific confirmation, it could be explained as the stepping stone to proving the existence of extra spatial dimensions.

Everything is in tune with the universe; we are opening our fourth chakra, the heart chakra, to access the fourth dimension. A higher energy boost from space enables us to increase our frequency. Humanity as a whole is currently moving from a physical realm into the energy of the spiritual realm.

Did you notice that many people are turning away from material possessions and focusing on living a simpler life in tune with nature? Today, there is a collective understanding of the fact that the materialistic world, which was imposed on us, was only enslaving us and blocking our spiritual growth. It's all part of the transition phase, which most of us are experiencing daily.

Those who are not experiencing it are most probably not ready to make a move into the fourth dimension. They will stay in a three-dimensional world until their consciousness and frequency level are high enough to ascend. They are not to blame or forced; we all have the gift of free will, it's their own decision, and we should not intervene.

As mentioned, we will alter our physical reality into a spiritual, more energy-based reality in our next dimension. It means that energy-based principles will replace former physically based perceptions and beliefs. We will finally start understanding that everything we see in the material world is conceived in the spiritual world. Thoughts and feelings are the creative tools of our universe.

The whole process of the shift started a very long time ago (at least in our earthly perception of time) and is speeding up at warp speed for the moment. As the frequencies increase, so does our perception of time. Didn't you notice that time is speeding up? It's all related to the increase of our consciousness level and the boost of cosmic energy sent to us to help humanity with the process.

Before moving into the next dimension, we must clear all issues blocking our spiritual growth.

What is happening in our world today must be exposed, but at the same time, we must find the ability to forgive. Not an easy task, but it's the only way to change our frequencies. All the material problems, diseases, relational issues, hate and greed, are all manifestations of the physical realm in the third dimension. It is time for us to learn about forgiveness and unconditional love, our key into the more spiritual, light energy-based dimensions.

# UFOs and interdimensional beings

We will investigate how UFOs and inter-dimensional beings can be connected to our increased consciousness.

Jacques Vallée, a computer scientist, astronomer and ufologist, was the first to advance the idea that unidentified flying objects (UFOs) are inter-dimensional. At first, he validated the extraterrestrial hypothesis (ETH); it was only much later that he explored the commonalities between UFOs, demons, angels, ghosts, religious movements, cults, and even psychic phenomena, that he changed his mind and defended the inter-dimensional hypothesis. (IDH)

Vallée found out that, what we commonly know as extraterrestrials, could come from any space-time and live amongst us, although remaining invisible in our current third dimension. He also believes there is human intervention, which he classifies as a secondary aspect of the phenomenon.

This joined human and non-human intervention is considered a way to alter human society by changing their belief system and suggesting it's an alien intervention from outer space.

According to Wikipedia, Vallée proposes that there is a genuine UFO phenomenon, partly associated with a form of non-human consciousness that manipulates space and time. The phenomenon has been active throughout human history and seems to masquerade in various forms in different cultures. In his opinion, the intelligence behind the phenomenon attempts social manipulation by using deception on the humans with whom they interact.

We will further examine the inter-dimensional aspect rather than the human and non-human manipulation to deceive humanity. If Valée is correct, the devices used can travel through different dimensions. It also explains why UFOs can be visible one moment and invisible a fraction later, the moment they leave our dimension. We could call it "materialising" and "dematerialising," it gives them the ability to appear and suddenly disappear from the radar. A phenomenon often observed with UFO sightings around the world.

The inter-dimensional nature of what we observe is another link to the existence of a "multiverse."

Dr Lisa Galarneau, an anthropologist, explains that; *"most extraterrestrial beings visiting our planet are extra-dimensional in nature, but limited to travel within and across dimensional realities within our sub-universe (there are many sub-universes in the cosmos).* She further claims that the UFOs we regularly see are inter-dimensional lightships that hail from a 5D reality into our dimension.

What is the link between UFOs and our rising Consciousness?

I would like to point out that we find convincing evidence of multidimensional creatures on earth and beyond; they are beings which manifest themselves at will. Sometimes they become visible to us due to fluctuations in the electromagnetic membrane, the element that separates our dimension from other unknown dimensions.

Jacques Valée said, *"We are dealing with yet unrecognised level of consciousness, independent of man but closely linked to the earth...I do not believe anymore that UFOs are simply the spacecraft of some race of extraterrestrial visitors. This notion is too simplistic to explain their appearance, the frequency of their manifestations through recorded history, and the structure of the information exchanged with them during contact."*

Many sources confirm today that we are not alone on our evolutionary path. We are assisted in our ascension into a higher dimension by interdimensional, higher evolved light beings. They are not necessarily the beings encountered in UFOs; the entities come from a dimension where no technology is needed to travel to our world or dimension. They have telepathic abilities and are composed of pure energy, enabling them to manifest themselves in any dimension, just by the power of thought.

We have often been deceived by reports from the Government, which are based on inaccurate and distorted stories about aliens and UFOs. They are actively involved in the reversed engineering of alien technology, hidden from the public for a very long time, not to help humanity but to control them. There is a cooperation between some alien beings and the shadow government, which the former put in place to manage.

Although it's known today that some aliens can travel through different dimensions and, by doing so, use their faculty to appear in our dimension, and disappear again in a split second without leaving a trace. To be clear, they are not the entities helping humanity but those trying to block us from moving into a higher dimension.

We must understand that only in lower dimensions "control" of the mind is possible. Once we move into more elevated, light energy dimensions, they will lose all grip on humanity.

As mentioned before, not all aliens are trying to have control over earth and the human race. Other light beings are willing to help us and give us the necessary knowledge to create a better world. A world which won't be governed by greed and ego, but instead by love and compassion amongst all life forms.

We should know that we are not alone in our ascension into the fourth dimension; a group of inter-dimensional beings assists us. They are referred to as the Galactic Federation of Light. You will probably ask yourself how we could know this. The answer is simple; we have a variety of witnesses, persons who were actively involved in different space and research programs led by the elite (Cabal).

There is one particular name which comes to mind when we talk about witnesses; his name is Corey Goode, an intuitive empath who was recruited through one of the MILAB programs (*Military Abduction of a person that indoctrinates and trains them for use in any "Black Op's Programs"*) when he was only six years old. Later he became involved as the interface to communicate with non-terrestrial beings in the Secret Space Program (SSP). After more than 20 years of involvement, he has been chosen as a delegate to speak with different ET Federations and Councils to deliver important messages to humanity.

According to Corey Goode, who claims to interact with a peaceful ancient race called "Blue Avians," those beings are currently assisting humanity with the ascension into a higher dimension. The same source claims they are a peaceful ancient race who entered our solar system aboard spherical ships. They came billions of years ago, and according to several witnesses, they are still amongst us today. This extraterrestrial race, which exists beyond the confines of time and space, is bringing us a message of hope and peace.

They told their medium (Corey Goode) that they have assisted humanity for thousands of years to increase our consciousness. It's a very long process because, as I mentioned before, we are given free will.

Goode described the beings as eight-foot-tall blue humanoids who are birdlike in appearance with bright indigo-blue feathers. If we look closer, they remind us of descriptions, paintings, and literature in ancient Egyptian, Indian and many other former civilisations. As a result of their higher density, they have extraordinary extra-dimensional abilities, far above our current comprehension.

These great spiritual masters are known for their bright intelligence and ability to raise vibrations around them. They can travel across the multiverse at will. The Blue Avians are thought to possess telekinetic powers due to their existence outside of what we perceive as our physical reality and dimension.

Corey Goode is not the only person they communicate with; throughout history, they spoke with Shamans, high priests and many advanced masters. Their level of intelligence has transcended physical limitations and duality, allowing them to act as a single intelligent entity.

It is said that their task on earth is to buffer and diffuse mighty waves coming into our solar system today. They can stabilise the new energy waves, which are responsible for helping us in our consciousness ascension.

According to Corey Goode, their main message to humanity is that to have the ability to ascend into a higher dimension; we should solve our problems first. Humanity has a free will to evolve spiritually or not; light beings will therefore refrain from intervening, except when they are specifically asked to help.

The current mass awakening around the world is a sign which indicates that humanity is ready to make the consciousness leap. The symptoms of the "pre-ascension" are all around us. The search for truth and the exposure of misconduct worldwide are all signs of a significant shift in preparation.

Many people wake up from a long sleep, a state which keeps them under mind control to serve those wanting to control and enslave humanity. While we slowly move into the higher dimension, the truth is being revealed, and we will see the true face of those trying to control us and the light beings helping us during this critical ascension. Soon we will be able to discover if people like Corey Goode, and many others who came with similar stories, were telling us the truth about their experiences. After researching the subject and receiving information from my spiritual guide, I am convinced that humanity is not alone but gently guided by higher spiritual beings who only want the best for us.

# The Akashic Records

What are the Akashic records?

They are a compendium of all human events, comprising emotions and thoughts that occur in our space-time, present, future and past. Theosophists believe that they are encoded in what they call the etheric plane, which is a non-physical plane of existence. H.P. Blavatsky referred to them as *"indestructible tablets of the astral light."*

Alice A.Bailey wrote in her book "Light of the Soul on the Yoga Sutras of Patanjali" that; *"The akashic record is like an immense photographic film, registering all the desires and earth experiences of our planet. Those who perceive it will see pictured thereon: The life experiences of every human being since time began, the reactions to the experience of the entire animal kingdom, the aggregation of the thought-forms of a karmic nature (based on desire) of every human unit throughout time."*

Some sources refer to the Akashic Records as being "*the book of life*," we could compare it to an enormous database kept in a special place in the universe. The most exciting part is that they considerably influence each being. Memories of past actions subconsciously give us directions in the present life. The Akashic Records are an essential tool to increase our consciousness and grow spiritually.

The famous clairvoyant Edgar Cayce said once, "*Upon time and space is written the thoughts, the deeds, the activities of an entity - as about its environs, its hereditary influence; as directed - or judgement drew by or according to what the entity's ideal is.*"

We could state that our reality is a consciousness hologram and that the Akashic Records refer to the hologram of consciousness grids that create our reality as we perceive it. A library wherein we can access all information.

The Akashic Records, which contain all there is, was or will ever be, are recording every event, intent or action of an individual or a group. They also keep a record of all changes to the universe. We could compare it to a super-computer, connected to each of us, reacting to what we do, think or feel, and changing our reality into what we create with our thoughts, feelings or actions.

The records not only connect us all, but they also influence human patterns. When we tap into them, we can find answers to our questions and find inspiration and knowledge on all levels imaginable and beyond.

The existence of the Akashic Records can explain why clairvoyants can see past, present, and future events in someone's life. It could also explain why we are often guided into some critical actions in our life, resulting in a positive or negative outcome, in line with the spiritual lessons we need to learn while in a physical form.

We create our physical environment through our thoughts and actions, including our interactions with the rest of creation. (material, physical or spiritual) Therefore past adverse events will always influence the present and shape our future if we don't take action to alter them.

An interesting example is a war - how many battles do we have to fight until we understand that they never brought anything else than destruction to humanity? As long as we don't learn from the past, events will be created to keep us in this negative experience. It's all part of the plan of creation and evolution, it might look evil at first, but in reality, it is the only way to increase our consciousness. We need to learn it the hard way until we understand it.

People often ask themselves why bad things are happening in their lives, and the answer is quite simple - they didn't learn or understand important lessons in previous lives. Whatever happens to them will continue to repeat itself until they see and understand why it's happening. Look into the past and learn and understand what went wrong.

Once you discover why bad things happen in your life, automatically, the world in which you live will change. We are all connected to the Akashic Records by enormous energy fields, which make up our living universe. Not only are our actions, thoughts and feelings registered in this giant database, but we can also tap into an unlimited knowledge base.

Did you ever enter a room and feel something was wrong or have a strange feeling that something happened in that space? Every being leaves an energy imprint that others can perceive, an energy that can transcend realms or dimensions.

A thought-provoking example is that of a couple who was interested in buying a house. The villa has been on the market for quite some time, and although the price was low, the real estate agent experienced difficulties selling the property. As we will find out later, there was a profound reason for it. During the first visit, in the presence of the real estate agent, the couple saw a beautiful house with a large and well-maintained garden; it seemed the bargain of a lifetime. They were very enthusiastic when entering the house, but the mood changed quickly when their happiness and excitement were suddenly replaced by a strange feeling of deep sadness and pain. They had no clue why they suddenly both experienced this feeling and decided to continue viewing the house.

When they walked up the stairs, the initial feeling of sadness and pain was suddenly amplified, up to a point where the woman asked to get some fresh air and almost begged to leave the house. After a short break, the couple calmed down and decided to visit the rest of the house, but couldn't get rid of the strange feeling of sadness and pain, which was omnipresent in the place.

The real estate agent didn't mention anything, but after she was gone, intrigued by their feelings, the couple went to the neighbours to ask some questions about the house. They were perplexed when they told them that six months ago, a man killed his wife and two children, after which he killed himself. The neighbours added that they found the bodies in the staircase. It was the reason why the house was so long on the market. It was the negative energy surrounding it which kept potential buyers away.

The real-life story demonstrates again that points can be felt as they leave a trace in our current dimension. When they emit powerful negative loaded emotional energy, like in the case mentioned above, it can be felt by observers in our dimension. It's just another example of how we are interconnected and how all our actions, thoughts and feelings are registered in the Akashic Records.

Although scientists are still unable to prove evidence of our connection to the Akashic Records, our higher level of consciousness can acknowledge it. Our physical body is surrounded by what can be seen as an energy field or "the aura." This human energy shell is composed of seven chakras or energy centres. Our human body is composed of vibrating energy, the flow of energies will therefore be vital for the well-being of our physical body system and organs.

It's known that the human aura can give us strong indications of our state of wellness, both on a physical as well as a mental level. It can also indicate the level of consciousness of a person, as our internal frequencies work in harmony with changing environments. We are continuously trying to align our frequencies with our changing environment. It is evident that Mother Earth is changing, and so are we.

We can plug into the vast universe database or read "the book of life" whenever we search into our higher consciousness. This is an ability that most of the humankind lost over time; fortunately, rising vibrations today allow us to gain access again to the long-lost knowledge in this three-dimensional world.

Have you ever wondered why some people are so talented in specific domains? Why can a five-year-old boy play the piano as a virtuoso? Why do scientists always find essential discoveries in their dreams or a state of higher consciousness? Why do we sometimes recognise people and places we have never visited before in this lifetime?

The answer to that question must be searched in the ability of some people to access the Akashic Records. We are all interconnected and part of the same "source." We can connect, which differentiates us from other beings in the universe. Some humans are better at reading the records than others, depending on their level of consciousness. As more people become aware, our global consciousness will increase, and the higher our vibrations, the more we will gain access to the universe's database. The knowledge contained in the source is unlimited, and we will need to access the information in different steps, all in line with our consciousness levels.

Our personal Akashic Records will influence how we go through this life on earth. For example, we could mention that stressful situations in the past can still affect a person in this lifetime and dimension. We could classify it as subconscious stress, something which we might not be aware of on a conscious level but still influencing our energy in a negative way today.

Health problems which manifest themselves today could have been caused by undischarged stress (unresolved problems) recorded in past lifetimes. The same phenomenon is known as Karma or the unresolved accumulated issues from former incarnations. When our energy field is out of balance, the effects will manifest in our physical bodies. This is also why some people don't understand why they have a specific medical condition.

Our current healthcare system is treating the symptoms, not the cause, which often results in recurrent medical conditions, even after successful treatment. They don't use a holistic approach to look deeper into the patient's psyche and are therefore unable to find a permanent solution to heal. When the cause of illness is found in past events, no physical body treatment will be successful. The solution must be searched in the spiritual realm and is to be found in the Akashic Records.

The knowledge of the existence of the Akashic Records is nothing new; they were accessed by ancient people of various cultures before. It was known as the source of knowledge of the past, present and future by the Indians, Tibetans, Egyptians, Persians, Moors, Bonpo, Persians, Chaldeans, Chinese, Christians, Druids, Mayans and Greeks.

The Akashic Records were also mentioned in;

- The book of life in the Old Testament (Psalm 69:28)
- The New Testament (Philippians 4:3, Revelation 3:5, 13:8, 17:8, 20:12, 20:15 and revelation 21:27)

In Egypt, the Pharaohs were advised daily by those who could read the Akashic Records.

It is known that the Druids of Scotland, Ireland, Wales and England could read the Akashic Records.

The Vedas of Hindus and the Sanskrit language were extracted from the Records. The Mayan civilisation retrieved much of its knowledge from the ability of its sages to read and understand the Akashic Records. It also explains why they were an advanced civilisation.

Thanks to our ascension into a higher consciousness level, humanity will better understand why time isn't linear but only a perception of the latter in our three-dimensional environment. As mentioned above, the secret of the Akashic Records was known for a very long time by ancient sages. They could tap into the library of the universe and, by doing so, receive a glimpse of both past and future.

Ervin Laszlo (Author, philosopher of science, and system theorist) developed a theory that connects the Akashic Records with our consciousness. In a more scientific form, he suggests that the quantum vacuum, which contains all elements of our history, is also an integral part of our consciousness. The vacuum state is the total energy and information-carrying field that informs not just the current universe but all universes past and present; Laszlo calls it the "Metaverse." It is also described as a collective virtual shared space created by converging virtually enhanced physical reality and physically persistent virtual space.

According to Laszlo's theory, everything in the universe has consciousness; not only we as humans, but also a cloud, a tree, or even a stone. Laszlo concludes that life happens because it comes from the quantum vacuum. We need to change how we view the universe and its creation.

Laszlo agrees with the Hindus, who claim that the Akashic Record is a field from which all the universe is formed; it holds all that ever was, is, or will be. He further believes that information can be transferred from one cycle to the next.

The Akashic Field not only flows through all the other realms of stars, galaxies, and human life but also the activating force that moves stars and galaxies. It's the spark that gives life to molecules and the driving power of the continuous evolution of our consciousness. It can be recognised as the force that shows us the universe's unity and total interconnectivity.

Ervin Laszlo's theory explains that we are linked to all people who have ever lived, and through the Akashic Records, we can get access to them. It would be a reasonable explanation for life after death, as the past has never disappeared and is still present in everything we do today. Once again, we can confirm that we live in a universe where all is one, and all is connected.

It would also explain why we can access what we call the "supernatural," which in reality is just "natural" when accessing the Akashic records. It can give us a clear understanding of clairvoyance, reincarnation and spiritual healing.

What is the link between the Akashic Records and religion?

Deepak Chopra explains, "*Spirituality is the experience of that domain of awareness where we experience our universality. This domain is a core consciousness that is beyond our mind, intellect, and ego. In religious traditions, this core consciousness is referred to as the soul, which is part of a collective soul or collective consciousness, which in turn is part of a more universal domain of consciousness referred to in religions as God.*"

Michael Beckwith said on the subject that; "*when you strip away the culture, history, and dogma of every religion, the teachers of those religions were teaching very similar principles and practices that led to a sense of oneness, that ended a sense of separation from the whole.*"

It has been the quest of all great teachers and spiritual masters to communion with this oneness. Scientists are still seeking the "theory of everything," which would account for all the laws of nature and explain everything that ever happened and will happen in our entire universe. According to Albert Einstein, this equation would be as reading the mind of God. We cannot explain everything from our limited three-dimensional plane, but we have enough indications to believe that the Akashic Records and our consciousness are linked.

# The "end of time" predictions

On December 21, 2012, the Mayan calendar ended after 5,126 years. Although the Mayans never mentioned cataclysmic events as the reason for what was the end of a cycle, many believed the date to predict an apocalyptic end of the world. Multiple doomsday predictions have been made long before 2012. Christopher Columbus was the first to think that the discovery of the Mayas would bring about the Apocalypse. Astrological predictions largely supported his belief. Some sources claimed that a planet called Nibiru, or Planet X, would pass earth or, even worse, collide with it on that date. It didn't happen as predicted; instead, a significant change in our frequencies triggered a mass awakening process, which is still ongoing today.

The approach of the Nemesis system (our binary twin star) triggered wide speculation that it could be responsible for a mass extinction event caused by a pole shift or a direct hit of the planet itself. The timing given by different sources wasn't correct and open to discussion.

There are other, more plausible interpretations regarding the end of time prophecies;

According to Ricardo Cajas, president of the Collectivo de Organizaciones Indigenas de Guatemala, the date didn't represent the end of humanity but rather the start of a new cycle of "changes in human consciousness."

The end of the Mayan calendar wasn't the end for humanity but rather the start of an era of expanding consciousness. John Hoopes, a scholar of Mayan history, said, *"A lot of the end of the world mythologies are the result of Christian eschatology introduced by Franciscan missionaries,"* and therefore, not part of the Mayan belief system. The Mayans saw the date instead as the end of an era and the beginning of a new cycle for humanity.

When Christians misinterpreted the Mayan calendar to create fear, they made a means to control the masses. It's a technique that many other religions would also use as a form of submission.

We can find the end of time in the eschatologies of different world religions. They all claim that the world will end in an apocalyptic final climax—a battle between good and evil, a time when the Messiah will return to earth.

Christ or Isa (Jesus) will face the Antichrist in Islam and Christianity. In Judaism, the end of days is part of the Messianic age and the coming of the Messiah. Even in Hinduism, they predict the final appearance of Vishnu, who will bring an end to the current Kali Yuga., which is the last of the four stages "cycles" the world goes through. (As described in the Sanskrit scriptures) In Buddhism, the Buddha also predicted that the earth would go through a face of turmoil, after which seven suns would destroy the planet.

Some believe that Jesus foretold the end of days when he mentioned that it will come like a "thief in the night," or in Matthew 24:36, in which Jesus has been quoted to have said: *"But concerning that day and hour no one knows, not even the angels of heaven, nor the Son, but the Father only."*

We can observe today that, unfortunately, our society has degenerated into a money-hungry, ego-centric community with little or no compassion and love for each other—a world governed by consumerism and a quest for lust. Most of us lost contact with nature and, most of all, contact with our inner-self. Psychologist Peter Kahn from the University of Washington claims that *"with so much life based on electronic representations of reality, humans risk losing touch with nature."*

Are the prophecies of religions coming true?

We can confirm that the prophesied turmoil and social degeneration are revealed today. Still, at the same time, we must admit that there is a sudden (massive) increase in consciousness, countering events in turbulent times. Humanity seems to be allowed to clear Karma and move into a higher dimension.

Maybe religions are too focussed on controlling people rather than helping them find their inner spiritual strength. Humans create religions to set regulations and rituals. Unfortunately, they became corrupt and are used to divide rather than unite people.

We experience a consistent increase in violence, corruption, and degenerating social behaviour in our society today. Still, at the same time, an increasing amount of people are known to raise their consciousness level. They are doing this by a process known as the "awakening," created by a rise in the Schumann Resonances and a flux of cosmic rays. The cosmic rays, considered extremely dangerous by scientists, are also directly responsible for our raised consciousness level. In a certain way, it confirms that the prophecies are correct when they mention that humanity will experience the end of time.

As with all prophecies, they are subject to interpretation and understanding. Religious people will have different interpretations than atheists, and therefore views might differ broadly. We can only account for what we observe today and make our own (subjective) conclusions.

Doomsday predictions are an ideal tool to create fear-based control over the masses, but the author leaves this aspect open to the interpretation and belief system of the reader. We will instead focus on what to expect in our new dimension.

Are the doomsday prophecies correct?

Reality fact checking indicates that most prophecies are highly subjective to interpretation, making them unreliable - at least, most of the time. Another less known factor is that nothing in the universe is static, and events can change according to conditions influenced by our collective thought process.

There is some kind of "constant" in history, which lets us experience similar events in separate time frames. An adverse event can only be avoided when we collectively understand the cause and change our behaviour, thoughts, and feelings. President Abraham Lincoln once said, *"The best way to predict the future is to create it."*

# The ascension

First, we must understand that there is no rush into the ascension, as each soul experiences its journey in perfect timing - only when it is ready will it happen without any significant effort. It's important to know that the soul must be aligned to a frequency which allows it to move from one dimension to the other comfortably. As long as we still see ourselves as a separate entity from the universe and other living beings, we are stuck in the third dimension.

The keyword is "change," both physical (DNA) and mentally; we need to change our habits, the way we think, the way we act, and the way we perceive the world in which we live today. We are not all on the same level of consciousness, making it a more complicated and sometimes painful exercise, as some people will be aligned, whereas others will be entirely out of tune. As mentioned before, not all of us will be ready to jump to a higher consciousness level and move to a higher dimension.

Humanity is going through some difficult times, our world is in complete chaos, both on a physical and a mental level, but like with everything else in the universe, there is a sense to what is happening. To appreciate the sunshine, one needs the rain. We need the chaos to open our eyes and reveal the great deception we live in today. It is necessary to go through a phase of complex disclosures to accept the change.

We were deceived in many ways; religion, politics, history, education, and even science - nothing is what they told us it was. Millions worldwide are seeing the truth today and trying to expose what is happening. Although the experience is painful for some and unacceptable for others, it's all part of our ascension process.

In the book *"Why the New World Order will fail,"* I showed that there are many signs around the world indicating that the masses are awakening. The most critical change we noticed recently is that people no longer want to live with the lies from politicians. There are rebellions worldwide against different regimes and various unlawful practices by the elite. A familiar feeling of justice is spreading worldwide to stop injustice and inequality. The sudden rise in consciousness leads us into another era that will bring peace.

The increase in consciousness allows us to clear accumulated Karma, personally and on a group level. Even Mother Earth will be cleansed by geological changes, perceived negatively by many, but necessary to the new earth. Always remember that everything is made up of energy, which can be influenced by our individual and collective thoughts, feelings and actions. The change will not only be essential to us on earth but to the whole "connected" universe.

How can we change?

All change should start by looking inside ourselves, not others. We are all light beings with the ability to look inside to find how we can change our consciousness and, by doing so, our reality. To ascend into a higher dimension, we must clear the heavy burden of the more dense physical body and prepare for the lighter spiritual body.

Change won't come easy, as we must master our thoughts and feelings. If we feel fear or anger, it will manifest itself in an amplified way in the higher dimension; the same goes for love, compassion, inspiration, peace and joy. We need to direct our thoughts to positive aspects; in this way, we create a peaceful environment filled with love and compassion.

The major challenge we will face is keeping our vibrations high, as our thoughts instantly create the reality in which we live.

Do we have to leave our physical body to ascent?

When the physical body dies, we are ascending into a higher dimension. Still, in this case, we can transform our physical body into a lighter body without physically dying.

With the return of our spiritual awareness, the illusion of being separated from the universe will disappear. We are living in exciting times, as the shift is not only limited to humans but all beings and the objects surrounding us. According to different spiritual sources, it will be the first time for humanity to experience a transition into a higher dimension without physically dying.

What is happening to Mother Earth?

Not only is Earth changing its frequency, but so is our entire solar system. The changes are already visible today and will increase until the whole system has entered the next dimension. The old earth as we knew her, still in the third dimension, will disappear for those in higher dimensions and be replaced by higher vibrational energy earth.

The whole transition is certainly not going unnoticed, and without any suffering, we currently entered a period of profound changes of both physical and geological nature. We are experiencing earthquakes, hurricanes, tornados, pestilences, famines, and even worldwide wars of an intensity which we never experienced before. (at least not within our three-dimensional knowledge and experience). They are all signs of the imminent transition.

When will we enter the fourth dimension?

We are not yet fully aware of the shift because our consciousness level isn't high enough to observe the transformation, but all of this will change very soon. The change started in 2012 in an ever-accelerating mode.

The global shift will happen when a solar flare like intense light covers the world. This event will instantly transition from one realm (dimension) into another. The exact timing is unknown, as time is not part of the higher dimensions. We know that it will happen when humanity is ready for it. The only element we know today is that we are close to that time. Many who reincarnated on earth today have chosen to be part of the "transition team," Those amongst us now came from higher dimensions to assist humanity in this crucial spiritual evolution process.

I am experiencing the fourth dimension.

The moment our consciousness reaches a high enough level, we will be able to see structures and creatures we have never seen before. Planets that were said to be inhabited by scientists in the third dimension will show unseen life forms and civilisations, which we never saw before because they were all above our frequency observation level.

What our eyes perceive in the third dimension is what you perceive as your reality, but that same reality is entirely different in other dimensions. That's why scientists have difficulty proving the existence of elements beyond our perception.

Susanna Thorpe - Clark, author of "Changing the Thought: A Book of Insight," wrote in an article named "The Bigger Picture": *"We are changed physically from carbon-based beings with two strands of DNA into crystalline beings with 1,024 strands of DNA (eventually) because only crystalline substances can exist on higher dimensional levels."*

An essential element of the evolution of our consciousness, which has often been neglected in the literature, is the role of cosmic rays. Cosmic rays emit high-energy radiation, mainly originating outside the solar system and even from distant galaxies.

Upon impact with the earth's atmosphere, cosmic rays can produce showers of secondary particles which sometimes reach the surface. Composed primarily of high-energy protons and atomic nuclei, they are of uncertain origin. (Wikipedia)

A spiritual guide gave the author the following information about the upcoming changes: The recent decrease in earth's magnetic field is helping us to receive the necessary cosmic rays, which are responsible for our upgrade in DNA. Our sudden awareness and increased consciousness after a long sleep result from this upgrade. Many of us, at least those open to it on a spiritual level, are open to significant changes in our evolution.

Humanity is waking up in a fast-changing world, a change visible on a social and a geophysical level. The political chaos we live in today is a necessary evil in our learning and awakening process. Despite worrying about earth changes, including the pole shift, they are essential for our spiritual growth. Mother Earth is helping us to connect again with nature and is helping us understand how we, and all life surrounding us, are part of the single source.

People need to understand that they have to learn not to fear death as we know it, as we are light beings composed of energy, the element that encompasses the whole universe. Religions have primarily contributed to a belief system containing a vision of hell and heaven, all to control people and submit them to their doctrines. However, in reality, there are no such things, only creations of the mind. We are all light beings on our way to the one source, "God" state, the highest and purest energy source.

To better understand which elements are crucial to our development, we will further examine the effects of the cosmic rays on human beings and their ability to change our DNA.

What is the influence of cosmic rays on our consciousness?

Andrew Collins, a history and science writer, who studied the effects of cosmic rays on humans for years, claimed that; *"The effects of cosmic rays on our genetics have led to mutations within the body, within the mind, the brain, that has altered our perception of reality...The correspondence between ancient cosmic ray levels, sudden evolutionary leaps, and human technology and art are facts."*

Collins was not the only one to have made this exciting observation; Carl Sagan, a famous American astronomer, wrote in 1973 that human evolution resulted from incoming cosmic rays from distant neutron stars, demonstrating how everything in the universe influences everything else. We find sufficient evidence to conclude that there is a vibrational connection between all living and non-living manifestations influencing our spiritual evolution.

In recent years we found scientific evidence in extracted ice cores from polar stations in Greenland and Antarctica, indicating that over the past 100,000 years, there were three periods with increased cosmic radiation. We will look closely at the fascinating findings of different scientists studying the subject.

They found the first evidence of radiation around 60,000 years ago, the second between 40,000 - 35,000 years, and the last peak about 17,000 years ago. Each peak lasted for a period of about 2,000 years. It is believed to have caused mutations to human DNA; even more, they could also have changed other life forms on earth.

We won't further investigate the creation of humanity as we know it today. Still, everyone should be aware of the impact of the cosmic rays on our DNA and how they could transform our consciousness level.

Are we being transformed into higher spiritual beings with the help of the universe, a transformation which will bring us one step closer to the one source (God)? The answer is YES; we are being assisted in many ways to achieve this next important step. Our DNA is being upgraded for the next level of consciousness, enabling us to transform our current physical body into a lighter energy body.

In an interview with the controversial Dr Berrenda Fox, who has doctorates in physiology and naturopathy, she confirmed through blood tests that some people have already developed new strands of DNA. Geneticists worldwide agree that our DNA is changing but can't establish what is changing.

Dr Fox claimed that: *"Everyone has one double helix of DNA. What we are finding is that other helixes are being formed. In the double helix, two DNA strands are coiled into a spiral. It is my understanding that we will be developing twelve helixes."*

By conducting tests on children with extraordinary abilities - powers, such as those who can move objects across a room by concentrating on them, or others that can fill glasses with water just by looking at them, she provided proof that their DNA is evolving and changing them into another, more spiritual being. Dr Fox is convinced that we are all evolving into this new human race with telepathic and what seems supernatural powers to us now.

The change is already visible; she further claimed that many of today's children already have magnetically lighter bodies. Older people may feel exhausted because every cell in the body is being renewed. It could explain why many people feel sick, experience mental confusion, or even believe they are going crazy. Often doctors cannot pinpoint the exact cause and just prescribe Prozac to alleviate the symptoms. Unfortunately, this doesn't work and usually has more side effects, aggravating the situation. The leading cause our doctors can't relate to it is because they are not used to dealing with the energy body, only the physical one.

Hidden to us is that we find an additional ten ethereal strands of DNA for every double helix with two strands of DNA. They have always been in a latent state; we never understood their natural potential for us humans until recent discoveries. According to scientists, not surprisingly, we only use a tiny percentage of our two-stranded DNA. The activation of new DNA capability is happening right now (in our lifetime).

Although the change is already happening, we need to be aware that our consciousness shift won't be given to us without a battle with those trying to control and enslave us, the entities trying to keep us in the third dimension.

Let's have a look at what techniques are used to keep our consciousness low;

Chemtrails, a part of an ongoing artificial weather modification system, are currently modifying the earth's climate systems. They use reflecting nano-materials and toxic aerosols to reflect sunlight and harm us. We saw evidence in the previous chapter that solar radiation, considered very harmful to humans, has another, often mysterious function; it is known to activate genetic switches for human DNA. The universe gives us an activation to upgrade our consciousness level.

There is an attempt to block the natural connection of charged particles responsible for exchanges between the lower and upper atmosphere. This is why they intervene; by controlling the rate of the charged particles created through the ionisation field as it enters into our lower atmosphere and reaches ground level, they maintain certain frequency fences of a lower vibration. By using advanced technology to control the earth's magnetic field, they can invade the "planetary brain," or the invisible force field that controls and influences every life form on earth.

It means that if they can control the earth's magnetic field, they can also control the mind. Most people are entirely unaware of this, but it has been happening to us for a long time.

The direct connection between chemtrails and the ability, or rather inability, to raise our consciousness is based on the following hypothesis; chemtrails interfere with neurotransmitter functions in our body; they are the chemical medium through which the signals flow from one neuron to the next synapses. (A structure that permits a neuron to pass an electrical or chemical signal to another neuron or the target efferent cell). Those chemical synapses allow our nerve cells to form circuits with our central nervous system.

Let's further investigate how and why they interfere with our nerve cells.

The objective of those trying to keep us in a lower vibrational state is to disconnect cellular communication within the human body. This disconnection can change how we think, perceive reality, and influence our energetic electromagnetic balance. In other words, it's disturbing the energy flow within and around the body, and by doing so, it is also blocking higher consciousness development.

The main reason why we experience physical and mental problems today is related to the fact that our bodies and minds are overloaded by artificial electromagnetic exposure. (5G will be the next step) Their objective is to block us from receiving information from our higher self and spiritual guides.

Fortunately, most of us are starting to grasp that we are all inter-connected to the universe (comprising everything within and outside our realm) and each other. We realise today that our thoughts and feelings influence the reality in which we live. A fact shaped by our own and the collective consciousness of our world and dimension and that of all other planets in multiple dimensions.

Did you ever wonder why something on your mind yesterday suddenly came to materialisation today, or the moment you had a thought similar to that of your partner or even that of a stranger you just met? It's called synchronicity, a phenomenon which will only increase in frequency as we move into a higher dimension. It's a sign we can talk into the global consciousness and further evolve to the oneness.

Once we become more aware that our thoughts are responsible for our reality, we will need to learn how to control those thoughts. Higher consciousness carries more responsibility for each individual, as reality will be created much faster than in a three-dimensional environment. It will be a new challenge for humanity to have a much deeper experience of the environment in which we live and how we interact with others.

To adapt to our new conditions, our DNA has been changing for quite some time now and continues to upgrade daily. Although most changes are not visible in a third-dimensional environment, they will become visible in the fourth dimension. We will all experience higher vibrational energy, which will enable us to communicate telepathically with each other and give us the ability to understand better our connection to each other and that of the universe.

Many of us become aware of what is happening; even if we don't completely understand what is happening to us, we are already focussing on developing higher consciousness. As a result, they become more self-aware. The veil has been lifted; there is no return or anything to stop the forward movement; humanity has already started the ascension into a higher dimension.

Our attention has shifted from pursuits in the material world of the third dimension into the quest for knowledge and spiritual understanding of the higher dimension. The ingrained belief systems, which kept us in the third dimension, are collapsing today. We are angry because we realise that we have been lied to and feel the urge to disclose all that is going wrong in the world; the agenda of the elite, chemtrails, religion, war, politics, etc…are all part of our Karma relieve process.

How do we know if we are still in the third dimension?

- We experience opposites, such as; good and bad thoughts, good and bad decisions, and good and bad people.

- We compete with others to prove that we are better than others.

- We seek happiness outside ourselves; things like money, material possessions, relationships, and all sorts of physical attributes (like the beauty of the body) are key to fulfilment in life.

- We believe that our thoughts only belong to us, the individual.

- We distinct ourselves by achievements in life, such as job titles, material possessions, and even family.

Our transition starts from within by questioning our old belief system, politics, religion, and education. We realise that we were lied to on all levels, and all this for a very long time. Our materialistic world is a trap to enslave us and keep us away from the spiritual being inside us.

Signs that our consciousness begins to awaken.

Wakefulness (a state of being spiritually awake above average levels) is the keyword that would summarise our new state of higher consciousness. It's a distinct psychological state in which we recognise a form of enlightenment. Those awakened don't perceive the world as they did before but rather look at it from a different angle. We could compare it to how indigenous people, such as Indians or Aboriginals, who live in harmony with nature, and the more materialistic Westerners, see the world. They will have completely different views of the same world.

Let's have a look at the different aspects, or characteristics, indicating that we are moving towards our new state of spiritual wakefulness (enlightenment);

- Increased Timelessness

Past and future are becoming less important for those experiencing a spiritual awakening. Their focus will be more on the "now" and less on past experiences or future planning. The present understanding is what counts, with feelings for people around them and full awareness of the environment and sensations of the moment.

Some people might even experience the eternal now, described by many mystics and even current scientists as the merging of past, future and present as the state of "Oneness." It's a shift in the orientation of time, also known as the "eternal now."

We realise that time is only a construct of the mind, while we experience the only reality in the now. When we stay in the present, our mind is cleared of all thoughts (positive or negative) of the past or future. We will experience a sense of expansiveness of time.

The transition period we live in today is full of sometimes contradicting experiences. While the Schumann Resonances are increasing, our subjective observation of time gives us the impression that time is also accelerating. This experience will continue until we reach a point at which time will disappear, and at that moment, we will find ourselves in the "eternal now."

- Connectedness and harmony

A sense of aliveness will take over our new worldview. Everything around us becomes alive as energy forms; we even see inanimate objects, such as stones, furniture or even buildings, as light energy forms filled with spirit.

Natural phenomena, which aren't biologically alive, such as clouds, sea, sand, etc..........., will be seen as filled with a light spirit. Spiritually awake people can see and sense the atoms, which are the building blocks of what they see. There is a feeling of perfect harmony in everything in the universe. It's an all-pervading spiritual force which gives us that feeling of oneness. It's the feeling and knowledge that all is connected and works in perfect harmony. We could call this "the oneness of everything" or even the "oneness of the universe."

- Inner quietness

Our brain is known to work all the time, and our mind is filled with thoughts. It significantly affects us, as it disturbs our inner world and is often the cause of keeping us in a low vibrational state. The constant flow of negative thoughts, worries we might have, and last but not least negative emotions disconnect us from the essence of our whole being.

Those negative thoughts often reinforce our ego and amplify our sense of separateness. When we ascend to higher dimensions, our minds will be less cluttered with thoughts. In the higher dimension, our minds will become quiet, or at least we can stand back as an observer, not being affected by it, and let thoughts flow.

- Awareness of spiritual energy

With our increased consciousness comes a spiritual awakening and full awareness of the spiritual force which pervades all elements, including all spaces between them. One could consider it a deep sense of a "living presence". In our new higher density realm, we will have a much better understanding of the "God" source and learn that everything we can imagine is the manifestation of that source.  We could call it all-pervading spiritual energy rather than just a presence within.

- Experiencing intensified perception

Spiritually awakened people can see the world in an entirely different way.  They will be fascinated by the beauty of nature and appreciate the sky, the sea, the landscape and all creatures within the animal kingdom.

Increased sensitivity will give us a completely different view of our world.  It looks like someone opened the shutters and let us experience the beauty of nature and everything surrounding it.  An experience which can undoubtedly be overwhelming initially but so rewarding once we adapt to it.

We can be in awe of simple things in life, such as watching a tree, a flower, walking, or even just eating. Our increased sensitivity will let us experience brighter colours and sharper surroundings, making everything seem fresh and beautiful. We will share more powerful odours than we know in the lower dimensions. It will be a mind-blowing experience that changes our perspective on where and how we live.

- Compassion and empathy

Our increased sense of connection will allow us to generate empathy and compassion, which is extremely difficult to find in our third-dimensional realm. We are not only feeling connected to other humans but also to animals and everything that surrounds us. In our new environment, we can sense what others experience. If they are suffering, we will sense it immediately and feel the urge or impulse to help them. Because we no longer feel separated, we will also be able to handle their pain, which is impossible in our current third-dimensional world.

We will become more connected and experience a shared sense of being with others. Empathy in a pure form gives rise to love and compassion for others.

Although very often misunderstood in lower realms, it's the basis of love but crystal clear in higher dimensions. Love is the most positive, highest energy form in the universe. With our increased compassion and empathy, we will be able to grow towards the higher energy of pure love.

- Decreased fear of death

One of the significant signs indicating that we are moving into higher consciousness is a decrease in fear in general, and more specifically, the fear of death, which is an ingrained fundamental fear. Death is so traumatising for us because we are afraid of losing everything we achieved and accumulated in this life - it suddenly creates an effect of meaningless in the mind. Many people still have this perception because they don't believe in the possibility of life after death.

With the rise in consciousness comes a better understanding that death is not the end of our existence but rather the dissolution of our physical body. We will also understand that death is not the end of our consciousness but a fundamental transformation of consciousness into a higher state of being. As we evolve spiritually, we will understand that our being as an energy form is immortal and that our physical body is just a vehicle.

- The ability to just "Be."


Unawakened persons will find the need to escape their continuous stream of thoughts by staying as active as possible to calm the raging storm of ideas in their minds. It is the main reason they feel compelled to seek distractions and activities by going out, travelling or working more.


Awakened persons on the other side relish solitude, quietness, nature, and inactivity. They often enjoy being outside cities, close to or on the water, mountains, woods, or wildlife. This environment is more desirable to find the inner spirit, a place where people find the ability to turn inward, away from the mad world and the turbulence of never-ending thoughts.


- Non-materialism


One of the most enslaving elements in our third-dimensional realm is the need to fit into a system driven by consumerism. A system forces and encourages people to consume and buy as much as possible to feed the economy. It's a way to make them work hard to feel appreciated, respected, and loved by society.

Once we move into a state of higher consciousness, our ingrained impulse to accumulate material possessions will fall away. We won't feel the need for wealth, status, career, and the necessity to show our achievements to others any longer. The insecurity we had before, our financial situation, and even our appearance, will ultimately fade away. Appearance and intellect will no longer be perceived as necessary; there is nothing to prove to others. The fragile sense of self, vulnerability and incompleteness will disappear when we understand that in reality, we are all one. We will be much more focused on what we can do for others rather than thinking about our status.

- Authentic life

Life in our current realm is still dictated by religion, cultural values, and a variety of expectations triggered by society. Most people are indoctrinated by a system which doesn't let them think for themselves; we are like slaves following their masters. The ego is still vital, as most people are just playing parts in life, hiding who they are as a person. They want to please or dominate others by pretending to be what they are not. Creating an image of what society expects from them is a priority in our current dimension. It's the main reason people have problems in relationships and work.

When we move into higher dimensions, we are more guided by inner-directed (intuition) feelings than thoughts. It will make us more independent from the current cultural system and values; in a way, we will become more eccentric or even rebellious in the eyes of others who are not yet awake. A life where we are not trying to please others by doing what is socially expected of us but rather live according to our sense of what is right or wrong.

Persons experiencing an increased consciousness will most likely wholly reject consumerism and all status-oriented values that once were so important to them. Elements like status and appearance are not a priority any longer. Often they will show no interest in following new trends, television, radio, or any other mainstream media news or information. People with an increased consciousness will instead concentrate on becoming independent from the current consumerist society and try to be as self-sufficient as possible.

Another critical element of changing into a more authentic life is the feeling of connectivity with nature again, an ability most people lose over time. Those in power today encourage it by creating big cities that group as many people as possible. Consider it another way of trying to block our ascension, a fact known to many indigenous people who live close to nature.

## - Connecting with Mother Earth

We will grow our vegetables, use alternative power sources, live in more environmentally friendly houses and walk away from the consumerist society to experience a new self-sustainable life in nature. It will allow us to connect again with our inner self and Mother Earth.

## - Lost group identity

When we are in the sleep state, we will identify ourselves with different social aspects; nationality, ethnicity, careers, achievements, and political affiliations, just to mention a few.

The best description of those experiencing a spiritual awakening feel is as a "World Citizen." There is no feeling of connection with any country, race, religion, or indoctrinated political beliefs; they are all replaced by a sense of global oneness, which boundaries set up by controlling organisations do not limit. They don't want to be labelled as socialists, democrats, communists, or feel American, European, Asian, or African, and certainly don't want to belong to any man-made religion. Some people could even call them rebels or anarchists because they no longer believe in the existing system.

- Newborn feeling

We feel as if we suddenly discovered a new person within ourselves. Awakened persons can make a sudden U-turn in life and follow an entirely different path than the one they followed before. Increased awareness from within gives an undiscovered view of all aspects of life and the universe in general. Our perspective and understanding of what is going on around us change entirely.

What makes awakened persons different?

Thanks to newly acquired freedom and release from psychological discord, they can think less about the future and ignore negativity from past experiences. It makes them feel more relaxed and less prone to negativity in general. Awakened persons have fewer problems with negative states, such as boredom, dissatisfaction, or even loneliness.

In strong contrast to non-awakened persons, those who have an increased level of consciousness will instead feel a great sense of gratitude about what they have in life and will not be craving for what they don't have. Appreciation is, therefore, a vital sign of what we call "the spiritual awakening."

Awakened persons have a great sense of spiritual awareness, an ability that gives them a much broader perspective than others. They will live in full respect of nature and make more ethical decisions when buying or using genetically modified or produced products in countries where they use children for the production, to mention a few.

They become more aware of the growing importance of burning global ecological problems while having a sense of responsibility and concern for social issues, such as poverty and inequality. There is a significant shift in how they see the world and its leaders; trust makes a place for justice. They will have a much higher sense of morality than before, which can be seen as a more developed, all-encompassing, unconditional type of morality.

A significant positive element in the awakened persons is their increased empathy and compassion, which makes them more tolerant and understanding in relationships with others. The fact that they no longer play roles in life, and are showing themselves precisely who they are, enables them to shift the focus away from themselves and give their full attention to the people around them.

# Life in the new dimension

The scientific angle.

Scientists recently published the conclusion of an experiment in which they studied the behaviour of light particles moving through glass which bounces the light rays back and forth between the edges. The scientists found irregularities in the behaviour of the light when simulating the effects of an electrical charge via physical input. They discovered that there was a fourth dimension working behind the scenes. Michael Rechtsman, an assistant professor of physics and author, mentioned that *"We have now shown that four-dimensional quantum Hall physics can be emulated using photons - particles of light - flowing through an intricately structured piece of glass - a waveguide array."*

Although scientists cannot explain every aspect of dimensions, in recent years, those involved in research on the subject came with astonishing results.

The conclusion after the experiments was terrific; the quantum Hall effect truly exists in four dimensions. Rechtsman said, "*This robustness of electron flow - the quantum Hall effect - is universal and can be observed in many different materials under very different conditions.*"

It's extremely difficult to explain exactly what to expect in the fourth dimension while living in a three-dimensional world. We can only observe two dimensions at a time, so we are very limited in our ability to move into or experience higher dimensions. Despite our current mental and physical limitations, some of us can have a glimpse of what is ahead. They can connect telepathically or spiritually to higher vibrational beings and planes (dimensions). As our consciousness grows, our ability to perceive and understand things we never could increase.

The account of our life in the fourth dimension, described below, is based on profound spiritual experiences from different people. What they all have in common is the fact that they are entirely in tune with each other, as all information was communicated to them via the same access channel tapping into the Akashic Records. We could compare this to different people reading out of the same book and telling the same story—the shift into a higher dimension.

Our dimensional shift, which has already begun, will be a smooth transition without what we experience as a physical death, which might be comforting news for many. Humanity's DNA is gradually being upgraded to include a higher vibrational state and a modified cellular structure. The human body will be transformed into a lighter physical form, which will be lighter in mass and density. It will be lighter because it is composed of light energy, which is less dense.

The difference between prior consciousness shifts is that the one happening right now encompasses our whole solar system and doesn't require any physical death for humans. The good news is that we won't have diseases like we used to have in the three-dimensional world any longer. Our bodies will be much lighter and healthier due to the higher vibrational state. Time will be something of the past, as we live in an environment that does not need any time measurement. The fourth and fifth dimension's description seems to be congruent with research on the human afterlife.

According to spiritual guides, the transition will be smooth, with visible human and animal behaviour changes—an exciting element we already experience today.

In nature, we can observe that wild animals around us feel less threatened than before or that people have become much more compassionate than ever. Some among us start seeing things we have never seen before, and those are not hallucinations but the manifestation of a higher dimension. They are all signs that we are slowly moving into our next dimension. There is still chaos and violence, but this is inherent to those who can't accept the higher vibrations - as it irritates them, they have difficulties adapting and fighting their amplified feelings. Those people will be left in the third dimension, slowly disappearing for the souls in a higher dimension.

It's our inner light, the connection to the one source, "God," which is responsible for changing our physical bodies. The transformation from a carbon-based cellular structure into a new crystalline form. Light energy is the force which is raising consciousness by not only taking man but our entire solar system into higher dimensions.

Imagine a world without crime and diseases, full of love and compassion, a world in which feelings are amplified, colours are brighter, and nature is more beautiful than what we have ever experienced before. We expect our bodies to become more youthful and healthy in the fourth dimension. It's all part of the natural evolution of our DNA.

The new DNA structure will be responsible for upgrading us to crystalline light beings. A fourth dimension is already a place where we embrace the power of our thoughts; more than ever, we will realise how powerful thoughts and feelings are. Telepathy, tele transportation, dematerialisation, energy healing, and last but not least, spontaneous manifestations will all be part of our new abilities in expanded consciousness.

We will live in a dimension which is free of toxic pollution of air, water and soil. A place of peace, where love and compassion for each other will be the new norm, a place where materialism, ego and greed don't exist any longer. The contemporary higher-dimensional society is nothing like we experienced in our third-dimensional world, as it only exists for the benefit and love of all—a world in harmony with all beings in all realms.

Many people who had the privilege of returning from a "near-death experience"(NDA) are talking about what they saw in the other dimension. The most exciting fact is that their stories concur with those of many other people who had similar experiences. Some among us manifest directly or indirectly the ability to look behind the veil, giving them a glimpse of what we can expect. They are the only ones able to provide us with an idea of what to expect shortly.

From our limited perspective, dying is terrible, as we leave our physical body behind and all our loved ones. Although we know that the body is only a vessel for the soul, we are still afraid of its biological effects and pain. In reality, we shouldn't be scared; dying is like passing from one room into the other.

We, as human beings, have been given a most beautiful gift, that of control of our consciousness. Humans are free to determine the level of consciousness they want to obtain while still present in their physical bodies. Each individual has complete control of their growth and evolution of consciousness. People often forget that they have a free choice to rise or lower their level of consciousness.

In the fourth dimension, and others above, much more than in the third dimension, our thoughts will shape our lives and the environment and reality in which we live. The world we will live in is the materialisation of the energy manifested by our thoughts and feelings. Our level of consciousness will determine what we create and how we deal with our collective emotions.

As mentioned before, the growth towards "oneness," or one source, will play an essential role in all higher dimensions.

As we discussed earlier, the universe consists of energy (vibrations), the same energy produced by our collective thoughts. This is why our thoughts are so important in a higher dimensional environment. The higher the dimension, the higher our vibrations and ability to instantly create our environment.

Increasing our vibrations is changing the Earth, all life forms, and even the entire universe. The process is not limited by time and space and is responsible for healing Earth with all the other multidimensional universes. Vibrations are energy forms responsible for our transition into the fourth and higher dimensions. Remember that we are all interconnected and receive the ability to create, as we are part of the same Source. This will become more evident once we live in the fourth dimension.

A feeling of oneness, the connection to the Creative Source of All, will fill our hearts and thoughts. It will answer many questions we still have today. We will discover that when we evolve into lighter, higher vibrational beings, we will also find that we are uniting in thoughts. More and more people are experiencing synchronicity, a sign of a collective thought process connected to the Creative Source. One of the elements which will disappear in the fourth dimension is fear, the low energy, which is keeping us away from any further spiritual growth.

The fourth dimension is an essential evolution toward a society where people respect and love each other. A world in which we show gratitude to Mother Earth. It will be the basis for our next evolution into the fifth dimension.

In the fourth dimension, our perception of time and space changes considerably when we better understand the past, present, and future. We will be able to feel the oneness without losing our egos. It's the last realm where physical presence (our body) contains individual consciousness. We are becoming aware of our multidimensional consciousness.

Our fourth-dimensional body has psychic abilities, something we never experienced before. Our intuition and creativity are much higher than we experienced before in the third dimension. However, be aware that there is also a downside to entering the lower levels of the fourth-dimensional plane, as they hold fear and negativity from the third-dimensional plane. We should try to create a positive mindset to avoid unpleasant experiences. A fourth-dimensional plane is a place where emotions are amplified and will manifest or materialise instantly. Thoughts and feelings will create our environment; that's why negative thoughts can develop fear or even evil and love beauty and happiness. Most of us will know intuitively how to deal with this.

The lessons we will learn in the fourth dimension differ from those experienced in the third dimension. We will need to learn how to live in harmony with each other, other beings, Mother Earth, and even the whole universe. In our new environment, there will be no need for money, and aggression or violence will become the evil of the past when the community takes care of all our needs.

Nothing in the universe is static; everything is dynamic and changing continuously in every aspect, entirely in tune with our consciousness level. We are evolving and expanding our consciousness into higher places of exploration, learning to let go of negativity, and creating full awareness of the spirit within us.

Some of us are already into the lower realms of the fourth dimension while physically still being connected to the third-dimensional realm. One of the signs indicating that a person is moving into a higher dimension is that he or she is no longer feeling attached to this world. People shifting into a state of higher consciousness are searching for solitude by trying to live outside of the cities, in complete harmony with nature. They can feel the negative influence created by the city's consumerism and ego-driven environment, wholly alienated from our natural surroundings.

Daniel J. Schwarzhoff, an American author, described life in the fourth dimension: "*Once we're reconnected, then even if we falter, consciousness immediately rises to show us our error and how to deal with each mistake along the way, in real-time. We make immediate restitution when appropriate, overlooking the cruelty and injustice of others without malice — conquering these with love as we face them moment-to-moment.*"

As discussed before, we are not living in a static environment but rather in an evolving multiverse with ever-changing realms, which are projected by the state of consciousness in which we are. By moving into a higher dimension, the perception of our reality will be completely different from one level to the other. Once we are in higher dimensions, we can still experience the third dimension, fortunately without the inconveniences of it.

We all have spiritual guides, although not everyone knows their existence in the third dimension. They will become visible in the fourth and higher dimensions to assist with the new living conditions. The guidance we receive is in the form of light, compassion, and intense feelings of love, the kind most of us never experienced in our current third dimension. Maybe it will be the first time (in a very long time) that you feel unconditional love so strong that you could easily burst out in tears of joy.

Our ever-increasing consciousness amplifies every feeling (positive or negative). It can be uncomfortable for some, but fortunately, we are not alone. Many spiritual guides are ready to help us in our new environment; we are blessed.

The subjective experience of the fourth dimension will differ for each individual, as we believe systems and cultural backgrounds might play an essential role in how we perceive each reality. Our religion might play an important role in how we perceive the new dimension. Many of us are conditioned by years of indoctrination by those trying to control our body, mind and soul.

# Conclusion

There is enough convincing evidence that not only humanity but also earth and our whole solar system are transiting into a higher density. We reached a critical crossroads in our consciousness evolution path. We could call it a point of no return; the ascension is one of the many miraculous events that will profoundly change the world in which we live.

Our soul has always been multi-dimensional; only our three-dimensional awareness blocks our consciousness's full extent and possibilities. It is also why we cannot observe beings or materialisations in higher dimensional realms.

Although scientists are coming closer to objectively explaining our environment's multi-dimensional nature, they can only observe the effects, not the reality itself. One needs to be in a higher dimension to understand it fully.

We have to realise that there will still be many things far beyond our current level of comprehension and therefore unexplainable from our point of view and reality, but it's something we just need to accept.

It is clear that humanity as we know it is changing into a new species with altered DNA, allowing us to vibrate high enough to live in higher dimensional planes. We can release fear and anger and look at those emotions differently. Thanks to a better understanding that all is energy, we will experience our reality entirely differently.

The author's perspective is that it cannot be fully understood or explained until an experience is felt and experienced in the higher dimension. Our brains aren't trained to see other dimensions; we need to learn how to use our third eye and complete intuition.

Below you will find some of the most critical signs; they are indicators that you are spiritually ready to enter the fourth dimension;

## 1  Questioning everything

You question all indoctrinated norms, rules, obligations, and traditions.   You realise that what you learned and experienced is not in line with the laws of the universe.

## 2  Authority

You developed a different view of authority, as you now make your own decisions based on your new intuition.

## 3.  Relationships

You become aware that sacrifice is no longer a requirement in relationships because you understand that they are only a means to acquire spiritual growth.   There is no feeling of possession any longer, just unconditional love.

## 2  The power of thoughts

You realise that your thoughts have a significant impact on your life. As a result, you will learn to use this ability to create a better environment.

### 3 Forgiveness - let go

Besides unconditional love, you will become aware that forgiveness changes your life's direction for the better. You can let go of all past negative influences in your life.

### 4 Fear

Fear and insecurity are something of the past; you will find safety using your thoughts and feelings.

### 5 The power to heal

You learn how to heal yourself and alleviate pain in your body. You understand the power of frequencies and the healing effect on your physical body.

### 6 Trust and intuition

You learn how to trust your inner guidance or intuition in all the decisions you have to make. Your intuition's power will also help you connect with the right people around you. Persons that will help you or contribute to increasing your vibrations and consciousness.

## 7 God

You understand that God, or the pure source of love, will not be found in churches, temples, or synagogues but within yourself.

## 8 Meditation

You are taking time out for meditation or enjoying quiet time to allow your soul to grow further towards the oneness state.

## 9 Releasing negativity

You are aware that negativity will affect your growth, so you would instead focus on releasing all negative thoughts and replacing them with positive ones. Let go of the past; it's essential to our spiritual growth.

## 10 Taking control

You can take control of your thoughts and feelings, allowing you to shape a positive environment. It will be a place that is entirely in tune with your emotions and expectations.

## 11 Time.

One of the most remarkable changes in the higher dimensions is our time perception and creation process. In contrast to the third dimension, you will experience that everything you want to do or create will instantly materialise.

## 12 Energy field

From a physical aspect, you will sense that the energy field in the higher dimension is much lighter and less dense. It's the result of an increased vibrational level.

We covered the main path in what can be seen as an extraordinary voyage into a new world which will bring us closer to the one source — "God."

The turbulent world we live in today, with all of its negativity, violence and hate, is only there to make us aware of the necessity to change our behaviour and path. Sometimes there is a need to shake people up to awaken them — this is precisely what is happening to our society today.

All the negative aspects in our world are there for a reason; they are a gift from the universe to open our eyes and understand that the change we desperately need is not to be found in others but within ourselves.

We are all undergoing a fundamental change; the following points are my recommendations to cope with the change;

- Accept your emotions.
- Acknowledge that change is part of your spiritual path.
- Be proactive and positive in every step you take.
- Reframe your situation to see the positive side.
- Try to meditate and connect with nature.
- Believe in the fact that you are assisted in the ascension.
- Trust in the one source, "God."

I am sending you lots of love and wishing you an incredible journey into this new enlightened existence.

Made in United States
North Haven, CT
05 February 2023